Solids & Liquids

Peter Riley

A+

Smart Apple Media

This book has been published in cooperation with Franklin Watts.

Editor: Rachel Tonkin, Designer: Proof Books,
Picture researcher: Diana Morris, Illustrations: Ian Thompson

Picture credits:
Kelvin Aitken/Still Pictures: 12b; Jonathan Blair/Corbis: 17t;
Jon Cancalosi/Still Pictures: 15t; Gary W. Carter/Corbis: 14tl,
29tl; Jean-Léo Dugast/Still Pictures: 22c; Simon Fraser/
Science Photo Library: 27; Ingram Publishing/Alamy: 25b;
Mark M. Lawrence/Corbis: 9b; Di Maggio/Still Pictures: 25t;
Gabe Palmer/Corbis: 11t; Fritz Polking/Still Pictures: 13c, 20b;
Secret Sea Visions/Still Pictures: 5cl; Jorgen Schytte/Still
Pictures: 4b; Janine Weidel Photo Library/Alamy: 26t;
Westend61/Alamy: 1, 24b; Michael S. Yamashita/Corbis: 17c.

With thanks to our models: James Cook and Gloria Maddy

Published in the United States by Smart Apple Media
2140 Howard Drive West, North Mankato, Minnesota 56003

Library of Congress Cataloging-in-Publication Data

Riley, Peter D.
Solid & liquids / by Peter Riley.
p. cm. — (Essential science)
Includes index.
ISBN-13: 978-1-59920-029-3
1. Solid state physics—Juvenile literature. 2. Solids—Juvenile
literature. 3. Liquids—Juvenile literature. I. Title. II. Title: Solids and
liquids.

QC176.3.R55 2007
530.4'1—dc22   2006030985

9 8 7 6 5 4 3 2 1

CONTENTS

SOLIDS AND LIQUIDS

Everything around you is made of matter. This is the word scientists use to describe all of the substances around us. There are three kinds of matter—solids, liquids, and gases. They are known as the three states of matter. In this book, we will look at two states of matter—solids and liquids.

These wooden blocks are solids. When they are stacked to make a tower, the block at the bottom holds up the other blocks without being flattened.

Because solids do not flatten easily, they can be made to support tall buildings such as this one.

Solids keep their shape

A major property of a solid is that it has a fixed shape. If solids did not have a fixed shape, how useful would they be? Imagine a wooden chair that changed shape when you sat on it or a cup that changed shape when you poured a drink into it. Many solids keep their shape even when there is a weight pressing down on them. They do not flatten easily. Can you think of any solids that you can flatten? What do you do to flatten them?

Liquids change their shape

The major property of a liquid is that it does not have a fixed shape. When a liquid is poured into a container, it flows and takes the shape of the container. Liquids also cannot be squeezed into a smaller space. This means that they can be used for support. For example, water beds have a mattress full of water. It supports people who sleep on it. Even some worms and slugs have skeletons made from water that support their bodies.

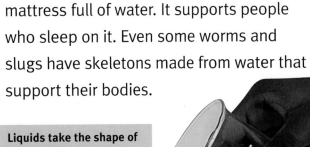
Liquids take the shape of their containers.

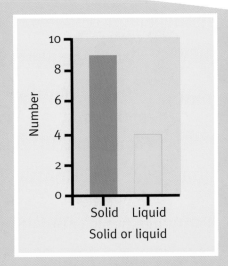

These slugs are filled with water. The water acts like a skeleton to support the slugs' bodies.

Use the data

When scientists do experiments, they make observations and record them. This information is called data. It may be recorded in a table, bar graph, or line graph. Look around you and make a list of all the different solids and liquids you can see. How many did you find? Make them into a bar graph like the one shown here. How does your data compare? Answers to the questions in this book are on page 31.

VOLUMES

Everything has a volume. Volume is the amount of space that something takes up, and it is measured in cubic inches. This is written after the value of the volume as in^3. For example, a volume of 50 cubic inches (819 cm^3) is written as 50 in^3.

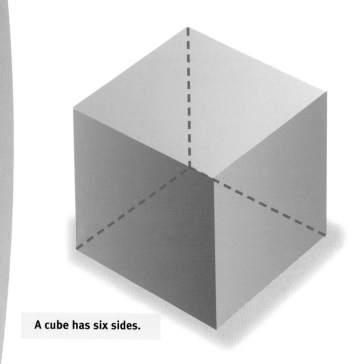

A cube has six sides.

What shape is a cube?

A cube is a shape with six square sides that are all the same size. Dice used for playing many board games are cube-shaped. If each edge of a cube measures one inch (2.54 cm) long, it has a volume of one cubic inch (16.4 cm^3).

Why scientists measure volume

Scientists measure volume to study the effect of things, such as heat, on different substances. For example, they may need to measure the amount of water produced when a cube of ice melts. Scientists also add liquids to solids or mix liquids together in experiments. To make sure the experiments work, scientists need to measure these volumes.

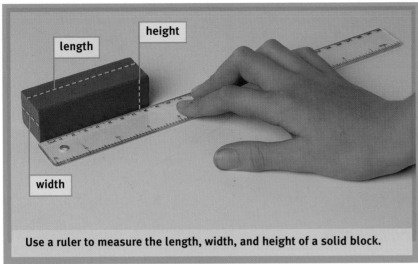

Use a ruler to measure the length, width, and height of a solid block.

Finding the volume of a solid block

Find the volume of a solid block. Measure its length, height, and width, then multiply them together. This block is 3.5 inches (8.89 cm) long, 1 inch (2.54 cm) high, and 1 inch (2.54 cm) wide. Its volume is 3.5 in^3 (57.4 cm^3).

Finding the volume of a liquid

You can find the volume of a liquid by using a beaker or graduated cylinder. There is a scale on the side of the container that measures ounces or milliliters. When you measure a liquid in a container, make sure it is at eye level. You will see that the surface of the liquid in the container turns upward a little at the sides. Look at the flat surface of the liquid in the center of the container to make an accurate measurement.

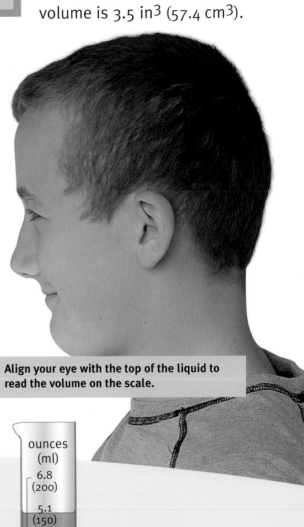

Align your eye with the top of the liquid to read the volume on the scale.

Finding the volumes

1 A wooden block measures 3 inches (7.62 cm) long, 1 inch (2.54 cm) high, and 2 inches (5.08 cm) wide. What is its volume?
2 What is the volume of liquid in this graduated cylinder?

ounces
(ml)

6.8
(200)

5.1
(150)

3.4
(100)

1.7
(50)

POWDERS

Powders are made from very small pieces of solids called particles. The small pieces are made when a larger piece of solid breaks up.

Powdered rock

Many years of summer heat and winter cold break up a rock into grains of sand.

Powders from plants

Grains of wheat contain a white substance that is ground up to make flour. The fruit and seeds of chili peppers are ground up to make chili powder.

Are powders like liquids?

Liquids can flow and be poured into a container. When the container is tilted, the liquid keeps a level surface. If a liquid is poured into a strainer, it passes straight through. Powders can also flow and be poured into a container. If the container is tilted, the powder moves and forms a level surface, but it does not do this as quickly or completely as a liquid. Powders can also pass through a strainer, but the strainer may have to be tapped a little to help the powder through.

When liquids are poured, they immediately form a flat surface.

Liquids keep a level surface even when you tilt them.

A powder can also be poured, but it forms a cone. The powder will form a level surface if you tilt the plate but not as quickly as a liquid.

Are powders different from liquids?

When a liquid is poured into a container, it forms a flat, level surface immediately. If a powder is poured into a container, it forms a cone. If a small amount of a liquid is poured from a jug, the liquid falls as drops, and a drip forms on the jug's spout. When sand is poured, a stream of small grains falls, and a drip does not form at the spout.

Powders do not splash or form drops.

The grains in damp sand stick together and can be used to make sand castles.

Powders can stick together

Water makes tiny particles of a solid stick together. Sand is made from tiny particles of rock that act like a powder. When they get damp, they stick together and can be used to make sand castles.

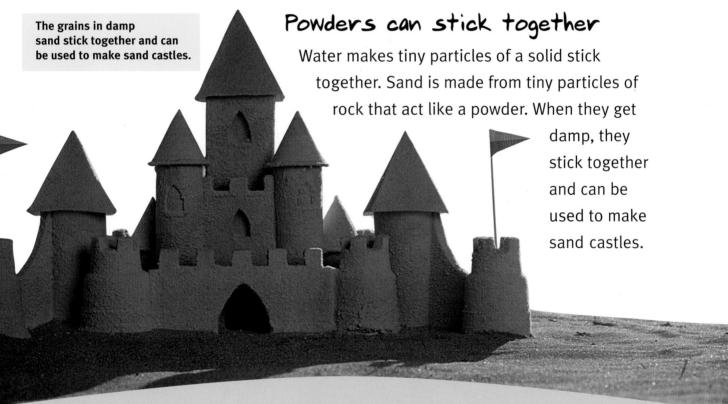

Soil particles

The tiny particles of solid in a powder are so small that most of them are measured in fractions of an inch. Here are four types of tiny particles found in soil. Arrange them in order starting with the smallest.

Clay	0.00008 inches (0.002 mm)
Sand	0.08 inches (2 mm)
Silt	0.0008 inches (0.02 mm)
Grit	0.008 inches (0.2 mm)

THICKNESS

The thickness of liquids varies depending on the liquid. For example, honey is much thicker than water.

water

honey

cooking oil

bubble bath

Testing the thickness of liquids

The thickness of liquids can be compared in the following way. Use a piece of material that does not absorb liquids, such as metal or plastic, to make a slope. Mark a line at the top where the drops of each liquid will be placed and a line at the bottom to show where the timing of the run ends.

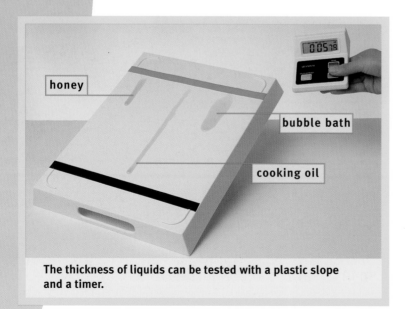

honey

bubble bath

cooking oil

The thickness of liquids can be tested with a plastic slope and a timer.

As soon as a drop of liquid is placed on the top line, start the timer and allow it to run until the liquid reaches the bottom line or stops flowing. Write down the time for the run. Test a second drop of liquid on a clean part of the slope. Repeat the test until the thickness of all the liquids has been recorded.

The scientific name for thickness

Scientists use the word "viscosity" instead of thickness. Viscosity means the resistance to flow. A liquid that flows quickly, such as water, does not have much resistance to flow. It has a low viscosity. A liquid that flows slowly, such as molasses, has a high resistance to flow. It has a high viscosity.

Thickness and heat

Liquids with a high viscosity change when they are heated. Their viscosity becomes lower, and they become more runny. Some liquids, such as motor oil, are specially made to run at high temperatures in an engine. The oil covers the moving metal parts and keeps them from wearing out as they rub against each other.

A woman checks the amount of oil in her car's engine.

Comparing how liquids run

Here is the amount of time it takes six liquids to run down a slope.

1 Which liquid had the highest viscosity?

2 Which liquid had the lowest viscosity?

3 Substance F was warmed and then made to run again. Do you think it ran faster or more slowly?

Liquid	Time (seconds)
A	14
B	6
C	10
D	4
E	12
F	7

MELTING

If a solid is heated to a certain temperature, it melts and becomes a liquid.

This chocolate is warmer than its melting point and has turned into a liquid.

What does temperature measure?

The temperature of a substance is a measure of how hot or cold something is. Temperature is measured in °F (Fahrenheit) or °C (Celsius). These are two different scales of temperature.

From solid to liquid

All solids have a fixed shape, and most, such as metals, have hard surfaces. When they are heated to a certain temperature, the hard surfaces become soft, the fixed shape begins to sag and flatten, and the substance starts to flow. This process of changing from a solid to a liquid is called melting. The temperature at which the solid melts is called the melting point. Different solids melt at different temperatures.

Liquid rock

The inside of Earth is so hot that it is made up of molten rock. At Earth's surface, the rock is cool and forms a thick, solid surface of rock. But at some places on Earth's surface, the molten rock from inside Earth breaks through. These breaks are called volcanoes. The hot rock, called magma, acts like a liquid and can even form a fountain. It forms a river of molten rock called a lava flow.

The lava from a volcano is molten rock.

Melting polar ice

There are huge sheets of ice at the North and South Poles, but changes in Earth's weather are causing them to melt. As they begin to melt, they break into huge pieces called icebergs, which eventually turn into water and enter the seas and oceans.

As these icebergs melt into the sea, they will cause the sea level to rise and some islands to disappear under the water.

Melting points of metals

Here are the melting points of some common metals.

1 Which metal has the highest melting point and which has the lowest?
2 What is the difference between the melting point of (a) silver and tin, (b) copper and gold, (c) silver and aluminum?

Metal	Melting point °F (°C)
Aluminum	1,220 (660)
Copper	1,981 (1,083)
Gold	1,947 (1,064)
Iron	2,802 (1,539)
Silver	1,763 (962)
Tin	449 (232)

FREEZING

Icicles form from drops of water that freeze.

When we think of something freezing, we think of water turning to ice, but other substances freeze, too.

Freezing process

If a liquid cools enough, it stops flowing and takes on a fixed shape. The liquid has turned into a solid in a process called freezing. The temperature at which this change takes place is called the freezing point. The freezing point of a substance is the same as its melting point.

Candle wax and lava

When a candle is lit, a pool of wax forms at the top below the flame. If too much wax melts, it flows down the side of the candle. As the molten wax moves away from the warm top of the candle, it cools until its freezing point is reached, then it turns into a solid.

Lava freezes in a similar way to wax. It flows from the volcano until it reaches its freezing point, then it turns into rock. Large drops of molten lava turn to rock as they reach their freezing point and fall as rocky lumps called volcanic bombs.

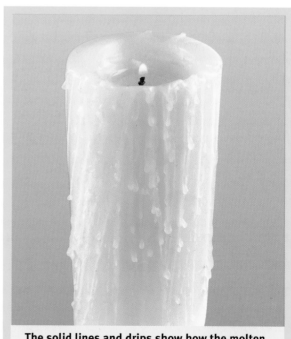

The solid lines and drips show how the molten wax flowed down the candle before it froze.

When this metal freezes, it takes the shape of the mold.

Powders from frozen solids

Clouds are made from tiny water drops that collect together. The tops of the clouds are so cold that the water drops freeze and form ice crystals. Normally these drops fall as rain, but in cold weather, they remain frozen and fall to the ground as snow.

Casting metals

When a metal is cast, it is heated until it melts and then poured into a mold. The liquid metal takes the shape of the mold, then cools and freezes. A mold is used to make the metal into complicated shapes, such as a car engine.

Freezing points

Here are the freezing points of six substances.

1 If the temperature fell from 86 °F (30 °C) to 14 °F (-10 °C), what is the order in which the substances would freeze?

2 Which substances would still be liquids at (a) 68 °F (20 °C) and (b) 50 °F (10 °C)?

Substance	Freezing point °F (°C)
A	52 (11)
B	77 (25)
C	63 (17)
D	23 (−5)
E	81 (27)
F	39 (4)

SEPARATING MIXTURES OF SOLIDS

Very small pieces of solids are called particles. If the particles are different sizes, they can be separated by sifting.

How does a strainer work?

A strainer is made from a wire gauze or mesh. If the holes in it are larger than some particles but smaller than others, the strainer can separate them. The particles that are smaller than the holes fall through them, while the particles that are larger are held back in the strainer.

Sifting in the kitchen

When salt or sugar gets damp, large lumps can form. The mixture of lumps and salt or sugar grains can be separated by pouring it into a strainer, then gently shaking it.

Sifting in the garden

Garden soil can have rocks and broken bricks in it. These can get in the way of the plant roots and stop them from growing properly. The rocks and bricks can be removed by placing the soil in a large strainer called a screen. This has holes in it that are large enough to let soil particles pass through but small enough to hold back stones and pieces of brick.

When lumpy sugar is sifted, the small grains fall through the holes, but the lumps remain behind.

Sifting on a dig

When archaeologists unearth the soil at a dig, they shake it on a big screen. Small particles of soil pass through, but larger items, such as pins, coins, and pieces of pottery, do not. They are collected and examined by the archaeologists to help them find out about people who lived in the past.

This screen is being shaken to separate the soil from items such as ancient pottery.

In some places, sifting flour is still done by hand.

Sifting at a flour mill

When wheat grains are ground up to make white flour, the powder in the grains is separated from other parts of the grain by sifting.

Strainers and particles

The table shows the size of particles in three different solids.

Solid	Particle size inches (mm)
A	0.12 (3)
B	0.08 (2)
C	0.04 (1)

There are two strainers available:
X has holes that are 0.1 inches (2.5 mm) wide and Y has holes that are 0.06 inches (1.5 mm) wide.

1 If a mixture contained particles of all three solids, what would happen when you used (a) strainer X to separate them, (b) strainer Y to separate them?

2 How could you use the strainers to separate the particles of the three solids?

WHEN LIQUIDS AND SOLIDS MEET

When solids and liquids meet, the liquids flow around the solids, and the solids may float, sink, or dissolve.

Dissolving solids

Solids that dissolve are called soluble solids. You can read about them on pages 20–21. These two pages are about solids that do not dissolve, called insoluble solids.

Floating solids

All solids have weight, which is a force that pushes downward. All liquids push upward on solids with a force called buoyancy. If the weight of a solid pushing down on the liquid is less than the buoyancy, the solid floats on the liquid.

grass

clay particles form a suspension

sand and grit form sediment

Soil is a mixture of solid particles that have different weights.

Sinking solids

If the weight of the solid is more than the buoyancy, the solid sinks. Its sinking speed depends on a force called water resistance. Large solids have less water resistance than small objects and so sink faster. Tiny particles sink very slowly and form a suspension.

Sediments

Large solids sink to the bottom of the liquid immediately. They form a layer called sediment. If a mixture of solids of different sizes is mixed with a liquid, the bigger solids sink first, and the smaller solids sink last.

Filtering

Mixtures of insoluble solids and liquids can be separated by filtering. A filter is made from filter paper. Filter paper has tiny holes in it that let the liquid flow through but hold back particles of insoluble solids. The filter is made by folding the paper into a cone, then turning it upside down in a filter funnel.

filter

sand

water

The water passes through the filter paper, but the sand is held back.

water

gauze

ground coffee

When the plunger is pushed down in the coffee pot, the water flows up through the gauze, but the ground coffee beans are pushed to the bottom.

Filtering coffee

Coffee made in a coffee pot is filtered when the plunger is pushed down. The plunger has a gauze similar to filter paper.

How do they sink?

Four solids with particles of different sizes are mixed with water. All of the particles have weights that are larger than the buoyancy. What is the order in which they form a sediment?

Solid	Particle size inches (mm)
A	1.6 (40)
B	0.04 (1)
C	0.4 (10)
D	0.2 (5)

DISSOLVING

If certain solids and liquids are mixed together, the solid seems to disappear into the liquid. When this happens, we say that the solid has dissolved in the liquid. Solids that dissolve are called soluble solids.

What happens to the solid?

When a solid dissolves, it breaks up into very tiny pieces, called particles, which are so small that they cannot be seen. The particles of some solids, such as instant coffee granules, give the liquid a color, but the particles of others, such as salt and sugar, do not.

Sugar cubes begin to dissolve when they are left in water.

Water flowing through this rock has dissolved parts of it away to make a cave.

Some dissolved particles, such as those of salt and sugar, give the liquid a particular taste, but the particles of rocks found in mineral waters do not. A liquid with a solid dissolved in it is called a solution.

Speeding up dissolving

Breaking up

When a solid dissolves, tiny particles of it escape at its surface and enter the liquid. A big lump of a solid looks as if it has a large surface, but if it is broken down into smaller bits, their surfaces are even greater. This allows more particles to escape into the liquid and speeds up dissolving.

Stirring up

If the water around the bits of solid is still, the particles move into it quickly at first. As they start to fill up the water, they move more slowly. When the water is stirred, it flows over the bits, picks up particles, and moves on. Every second a new portion of water sweeps by the bits and takes away the particles.

Stirring coffee granules helps dissolve them into the water.

Heating up

When solids warm, the tiny particles in them shake very slightly. If the solid is in a liquid, the particles at its surface shoot off quickly into the liquid and dissolve. The hotter the solid and liquid, the faster the solid dissolves.

Solubility

The solubility of a solid is found by measuring the mass of it that will dissolve in 6 in^3 (100 cm^3) of water. The higher the mass that dissolves, the higher the solubility.

1 Which solid is the most soluble?

2 Which solid is the least soluble?

3 (a) Is D more soluble than A?

(b) Is C more soluble than B?

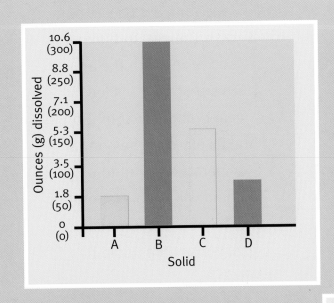

SEPARATING SOLUBLE SOLIDS

The particles of a dissolved solid can be separated from liquid by evaporation or chromatography, a technique used to separate substances.

Going through the holes

A filter paper cannot be used to separate a liquid from the solid particles dissolved in it. The particles are smaller than the holes in the paper and pass through them with the liquid.

Evaporation

Tiny particles break off from the surface of a liquid and form a gas (see page 24). The gas spreads out and mixes with the air. This process is called evaporation. Evaporation takes place at the normal temperatures around us.
A liquid will keep evaporating until all of it has turned into a gas. We say the liquid has dried up.

Seawater contains large amounts of dissolved salt. When it is placed in shallow pans and allowed to evaporate, the salt is left behind. These women are collecting the salt.

Leaving the solid behind

Solids cannot evaporate. If a solid is dissolved in a liquid, its particles stay behind while the liquid particles evaporate. Eventually, there is not enough liquid around the solid particles to keep them dissolved, so they turn back into a solid.

Chromatography

Chromatography can be used to separate a number of different soluble solids from their solution. A filter paper is used to carry the solution. As the liquid moves up through the filter paper, the solids that do not dissolve very well settle out on the paper first, and the solids that dissolve very well settle last. If the solids have different colored dyes, they form colored patches as they settle.

The different dyes in the ink settle out on the paper, showing the colors mixed to make the ink.

Time to evaporate

Some water was put into saucers and left to evaporate at different temperatures.

1 What happens to the way water evaporates as it gets warmer?

2 If you wanted to make the water evaporate more quickly than three days, what should you do?

Temperature °F (°C)	Evaporation time (days)
40 (5)	12
50 (10)	9
60 (15)	6
70 (21)	3

WHEN SOLIDS AND LIQUIDS CHANGE

Solids and liquids take part in two kinds of changes. These are called reversible and irreversible changes.

Reversible changes

When a solid is heated, it melts and turns into a liquid. This change is reversible because when the liquid cools, it freezes and turns back into a solid.

As the water boils, it changes into a gas.

What we often think is steam coming from a hot drink is actually condensed water droplets.

When water evaporates, it forms a gas called water vapor. This change is reversed when the water vapor changes back into a liquid again in a process called condensation. When a liquid is heated very strongly, bubbles form in it and rise to its surface. The hot, bubbling liquid is said to be boiling. The temperature at which a liquid boils is called its boiling point. As a liquid boils, it changes into a gas. Boiling is reversed when the gas cools and changes back into a liquid through condensation.

Irreversible changes

If a solid such as wood is heated very strongly, it burns. During the burning process, flames rise from the wood, and it changes into a substance called ash. Some of the wood turns into particles that rise in the air and make smoke. Smoke is formed when a substance in the wood, called carbon, takes part in a change with a gas in the air, called oxygen. They make a new gas called carbon dioxide. If ash, smoke, and carbon dioxide are put together, they do not make wood again. This is why burning is an irreversible change.

The burning wood gives off light and heat.

Egg whites take part in an irreversible change when they are heated.

When some substances get hot, they do not burn; they change in another way. Egg white is a clear liquid, but when it is heated in a pan, it becomes cloudy and white, then changes into a solid.

The three states of zinc

Here are the melting and boiling points of a metal called zinc, which is used to make buckets and battery cases.

Zinc has a melting point of 788 °F (420 °C) and a boiling point of 1,450 °F (788 °C).

Imagine zinc at each of these temperatures:

A 68 °F (20 °C); B 1,474 °F (801 °C); C 932 °F (500 °C)

At which temperature was zinc (a) a solid, (b) a liquid, (c) a gas?

NEW SUBSTANCES

When an irreversible change takes place, a new material is formed. The new material has different properties than the substances from which it is made. Many materials we use are made this way.

The clay hardens when it is heated at a high temperature.

Pottery

Clay is a soft solid that can be molded and pressed to make many kinds of shapes. When it is put in a kiln and heated to more than 1,470 °F (800 °C), it hardens to form pottery. The shape of a piece of pottery cannot be changed. If it falls on the floor, it does not just flatten like clay, but shatters into many pieces. We use pottery for cups, bowls, plates, and jars.

Concrete

Cement is a powder used to make concrete. It is mixed with water and other substances and can be poured. It hardens to make concrete, which cannot be changed.

Concrete is made in a concrete mixer and then poured out.

Plaster of Paris

If a person has a broken arm or leg, it is treated by covering it in a bandage coated in plaster of Paris. Plaster of Paris is a white powder that, when water is added to it, forms a creamy mixture that hardens into a white solid. If you could look at the solid with a microscope, you would see that the tiny fragments of powder had formed crystals that locked together like the pieces in a jigsaw puzzle to make the new substance hard.

Plastic

The plastics that we use today are made from substances in oil and natural gas. One substance is called ethylene. It is a gas, but when it is heated strongly and flattened, it changes into a new solid substance that scientists called polyethylene. It is used to make bags, bottles, and bowls.

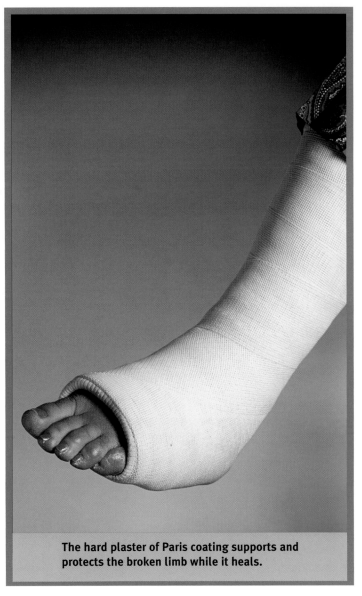

The hard plaster of Paris coating supports and protects the broken limb while it heals.

Reversible and irreversible changes

Here are some observations on changes.
Which changes have formed a new substance?

A. Hot dough turns into bread.
B. Warm butter turns into a liquid.
C. Slices of bread get a brown coating in a toaster.

CAN YOU REMEMBER THE ESSENTIALS?

Here are the essential science facts about solids and liquids. They are presented in the order you read about them in the book. Spend a couple of minutes learning each set of facts. If you can learn them all, you know all of the essentials about two states of matter—solids and liquids.

Volumes (pages 6–7)

The volume is the amount of space that a thing takes up. Volumes are measured in cubic inches (in ^{3}).
A beaker or graduated cylinder is used to measure the volume of a liquid.
The volume of a block can be found by measuring its length, height, and width and multiplying them together.

Thickness (pages 10–11)

The thickness of a liquid can be tested by timing how long it takes to run down a slope.
The scientific word for thickness is viscosity.
A liquid with a low viscosity runs quickly.
A liquid with a high viscosity runs slowly.
When a liquid is heated, its viscosity becomes lower.

Powders (pages 8–9)

A powder is made from very small pieces of a solid.
Very small pieces of a solid are called particles.
Sand and flour act like powders.
Powders can be poured.
Powders do not form drops.
Powders do not spread out when poured but form a cone.

Melting (pages 12–13)

If a solid is heated strongly enough, it melts.
A solid turns into a liquid when it melts.
The temperature at which a solid melts is called its melting point.

Freezing (pages 14-15)

If a liquid is cooled enough, it freezes. When a liquid freezes, it turns into a solid. The temperature at which a liquid freezes is called its freezing point.
The freezing point is the same as the melting point.

Dissolving (pages 20-21)

Solids that dissolve in a liquid are called soluble solids.
A liquid with a solid dissolved in it is called a solution.
Soluble solids can give a solution color and taste.
The very tiny pieces of solid that dissolve are called particles. Remember that this word is also used for small pieces of solids, such as grains of sand.
Dissolving can be sped up by breaking up the solid into small pieces, stirring, or warming the liquid.

Separating mixtures of solids (pages 16-17)

A strainer has holes in it. A strainer can be used to separate solids that have particles of different sizes. Small particles pass through the holes in a strainer. Large particles cannot pass through the holes in a strainer.

Separating soluble solids (pages 22-23)

Particles of a dissolved solid can be separated from a liquid by evaporation.
When a liquid evaporates, it turns into a gas.
Solids cannot evaporate.
In chromatography, solid particles settle out on a filter paper as the liquid soaks through it.

When liquids and solids meet (pages 18-19)

Solids that dissolve in a liquid are said to be soluble. Solids that do not dissolve in a liquid are said to be insoluble.

When insoluble solids mix with a liquid, they may float, form a suspension, or form a sediment.
Insoluble solids can be separated from a liquid by filtering.

When solids and liquids change (pages 24-25)

If a substance takes part in a reversible change, it can be changed back again.
Melting, freezing, evaporating and condensing, and boiling and condensing are reversible changes.
The temperature at which a liquid boils is called its boiling point.
If a substance takes part in an irreversible change, it cannot be changed back again.
Irreversible changes take place when a substance burns or is cooked.

New substances (pages 26-27)

A new substance is made when an irreversible change takes place.
The new substance has different properties from the substances that took part in the irreversible change.

GLOSSARY

Archaeologist A person who studies the past by examining the things people made and used.

Buoyancy The force of a liquid pushing upward on an object that has entered it.

Chemical reaction A change that takes place between two or more substances that cannot be reversed.

Chromatography The separation of colored substances dissolved in a liquid by allowing them to flow through paper with small holes in it.

Condensation A process in which a gas turns into a liquid when it cools.

Crystals Solids with a number of flat sides that are arranged at certain angles to one another.

Dissolve A process in which a substance separates and spreads out through a liquid and seems to disappear into it.

Evaporation A process in which a liquid changes into a gas at a temperature below the boiling point of the liquid.

Freezing A process in which a liquid changes into a solid.

Freezing point The temperature at which a liquid changes into a solid.

Gases Substances that do not have any certain shape or volume.

Insoluble solids Solids that will not dissolve in a liquid.

Irreversible change A change that takes place when a material changes and cannot be turned back again to the original material.

Melting A process in which a solid changes into a liquid.

Melting point The temperature at which a solid melts and changes into a liquid.

Metal A substance with a surface that conducts both heat and electricity well.

Plastic A solid material made from oil and gas that can be heated and molded into many shapes.

Property A special feature that a material possesses, such as having a high viscosity or a low melting point.

Reversible change A change that can be reversed. For example, melting is reversed by freezing, and evaporating is reversed by condensing.

Sediment The layer of insoluble solids that settle out at the bottom of a liquid when the liquid and the solids have been mixed together.

Solubility The amount of a substance that will dissolve in a certain amount of a liquid.

Soluble solids Solids that dissolve in a liquid.

Solution A liquid in which a substance has dissolved.

Suspension A large number of tiny solid particles that appear to float in a liquid but are actually slowly sinking.

Temperature The measure of the hotness or the coldness of a substance.

Viscosity The property of a liquid related to how fast it flows. A liquid with a high viscosity flows slowly; a liquid with a low viscosity flows quickly.

Weight The force of an object pressing down toward the center of Earth as a result of gravity.

ANSWERS

Volumes (pages 6–7)
1 6 in³ (98.3 cm³)
2 5.1 ounces (150 ml)

Powders (pages 8–9)
Clay, silt, grit, sand.

Thickness (pages 10–11)
1 A
2 D
3 It ran faster.

Melting (pages 12–13)
1 Iron has the highest; tin has the lowest.
2 (a) 1,314 °F (730 °C), (b) 34 °F (19 °C),
(c) 543 °F (302 °C).

Freezing (pages 14–15)
1 E, B, C, A, F, D.
2 (a) A, C, D, and F (b) D and F.

Separating mixtures of solids (pages 16–17)
1 (a) Solids B and C would pass through strainer X, and solid A would be left in the strainer; (b) solid C would pass through strainer Y, but solids A and B would be left in the strainer.
2 Use strainer X to separate A from B and C, then use strainer Y to separate B and C.

When solids and liquids meet (pages 18–19)
A sinks first, then C, D, and B.

Dissolving (pages 20–21)
1 B
2 A
3 (a) Yes; (b) No.

Separating soluble solids (pages 22–23)
1 As it gets warmer, the water evaporates faster.
2 Put it somewhere warmer than 70 °F (21 °C).

When solids and liquids change (pages 24–25)
(a) A; (b) C; (c) B.

New substances (pages 26–27)
A and C

INDEX